FIRST PEOPLES

THE AINU

OF JAPAN

BARBARA AOKI POISSON

Lerner Publications Company • Minneapolis

**First American edition published in 2002
by Lerner Publications Company**

Published by arrangement with Times Editions
Copyright © 2002 by Times Media Private Limited

Lerner Publications Company
A division of Lerner Publishing Group
241 First Avenue North
Minneapolis, MN 55401 U.S.A.
Website address: www.lernerbooks.com

Series originated and designed by
Times Editions
An imprint of Times Media Private Limited
A member of the Times Publishing Group
1 New Industrial Road, Singapore 536196
Website address: www.timesone.com.sg/te

Series editors: Margaret J. Goldstein, Yumi Ng
Series designers: Tuck Loong, Geoslyn Lim
Series picture researcher: Susan Jane Manuel

Library of Congress Cataloging-in-Publication Data
Poisson, Barbara Aoki.
The Ainu of Japan / by Barbara Aoki Poisson.— 1st American ed.
p. cm. — (First peoples)
Includes bibliographical references and index.
Summary: Describes the history, modern and traditional cultural practices and economies, geographic background, and ongoing oppression and struggles of the Ainu.
ISBN 0-8225-4176-9 (lib. bdg. : alk. paper)
1. Ainu—Juvenile literature. [1. Ainu.] I. Title. II. Series.
DS832 .P65 2002
952'.004946—dc21   2001004295

Printed in Malaysia
Bound in the United States of America

1 2 3 4 5 6—OS—07 06 05 04 03 02

CONTENTS

WHO ARE THE AINU?

The Ainu are the native people of Japan. They have shared their homeland with the Japanese people for centuries. Modern-day Ainu live much like other Japanese people do. But, in ancient times, the Ainu and the Japanese looked and lived very differently. The Ainu had curly hair and light skin. Ainu men grew beards. Ainu women painted tattoos on their faces. The Japanese, on the other hand, had straight hair and darker skin. Japanese men usually did not have facial hair. Over the years, many Ainu married Japanese. Their children did not always look Ainu. In modern times, full-blooded Ainu people are very rare. However, a few Ainu people still resemble their ancestors.

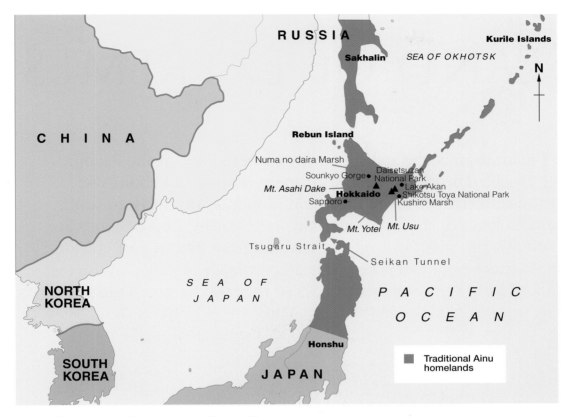

Traditional Homelands

Most Ainu people live on Hokkaido, the northernmost of Japan's four major islands. The Ainu called the island Ainu Moshir, meaning "peaceful land of humans" or "Ainu homeland." *Ainu* means "human" or "the people" in their language. A small number of Ainu lived on the northern part of Honshu, Japan's main island, and on the islands of Kurile and Sakhalin, which belong to Russia.

HOW MANY?

It's hard to find out how many Ainu (*right*) live in Japan. Since the Ainu have been treated unfairly, many of them do not want to reveal their heritage. In addition, most Ainu people have ancestors who are not just Ainu but are also Japanese or members of other groups. According to Cultural Survival, an international organization, around 200,000 Ainu people live in Japan. But the Japanese government estimates that only 25,000 Ainu live in Japan, according to a survey taken in 1986. The actual Ainu population remains a mystery.

LAND OF EXTREMES

Japan is an island nation on the western edge of the Pacific Ocean. The country has four main islands and about two thousand smaller ones. The main islands, from north to south, are Hokkaido, Honshu, Shikoku, and Kyushu. These islands are actually the peaks of underwater volcanoes. Because of volcanic activity, the ground is very unstable in Japan. Many earthquakes and tidal waves, or tsunamis, occur there every year. Volcanic eruptions are also common in Japan.

Below: The landscape of Rebun Island, off the northwestern tip of Hokkaido

Above: The Sounkyo Gorge in Hokkaido

Remote Island of the North

Hokkaido is surrounded by several bodies of water. The Pacific Ocean lies to the east and south. The Sea of Japan lies to the west. The Sea of Okhotsk lies to the north. The Tsugaru Strait separates Hokkaido from Honshu. In the past, people traveled on ferryboats to cross the deep waters of the Tsugaru Strait. In 1971, the Japanese began building the Seikan Tunnel, an underwater tunnel linking Hokkaido and Honshu. The tunnel was completed in 1988. At 33.5 miles (54 kilometers) long, it is the longest railroad tunnel and the longest underwater tunnel in the world.

Cool Climate

The temperatures on Hokkaido vary by region. The island's western coast is generally warmer than the eastern coast. Winters are cold and snowy. Some parts of Hokkaido get up to 20 feet (6 meters) of snow each year. In central Hokkaido, the average temperature in January is only 16 degrees Fahrenheit (-9 degrees Celsius). Summers are cool and dry. Even during August, the warmest month, temperatures in central Hokkaido average only 70 degrees Fahrenheit (21 degrees Celsius).

LET IT SNOW!

Sapporo, Hokkaido's capital city, hosts the Sapporo Snow Festival every February. The festival turns the city into a magical place. People build gigantic cartoon characters out of snow and copies of famous buildings made of ice. Children play on huge snow slides (*right*). At night, the displays sparkle with colorful lights. Millions of people from all over the world come to Sapporo to join in the festivities each year.

THE HOKKAIDO LANDSCAPE

Hokkaido is blessed with a beautiful landscape. It is home to rugged mountains, thick forests, rocky cliffs, colorful meadows, roaring waterfalls, and other natural wonders.

The Coasts

Hokkaido's coastline includes rugged cliffs, gentle hills, and sandy and rocky beaches. Typical plants along the coast include heather, a kind of shrub, and pine, fir, and spruce trees. Japanese pines are plentiful along the coasts, growing even on rocky cliffs.

Above: Kinshi waterfall slides down the rugged cliffs of Sounkyo Gorge.

Below: Autumn foliage covers the mountains of the Daisetsuzan.

The Mountains

Several mountain ranges run down the center of Hokkaido. The Daisetsuzan range is nicknamed "the roof of Hokkaido." It has many mountains over 6,500 feet (1,980 meters) high. Daisetsuzan National Park is home to Mount Asahi Dake, the tallest mountain in Hokkaido at 7,513 feet (2,290 meters).

Above: Numa no daira Marsh is located in Daisetsuzan National Park.

The Wetlands

Each spring, the snow begins to melt in the mountains. Water flows down to the lowlands, creating swamps, lakes, and marshes. These wetlands provide homes to many plants and animals. Kushiro Marsh in eastern Hokkaido is the largest wetland area in Japan. About two thousand species of plants and animals live in the marsh. It is a protected wildlife area, which means people cannot disturb the plants and animals there.

THE KING OF VOLCANOES

Japan has more than 150 major volcanoes. More than sixty of them are active, which means they frequently erupt. Mount Usu (*below*), located in Shikotsu Toya National Park in Hokkaido, is called "the king of volcanoes." Usu erupted on April 1, 2000, sending molten rock and volcanic ash 2 miles (3.2 kilometers) into the sky. Fortunately, nobody was hurt.

NATURE'S BOUNTY

Above: The ancient Ainu revered Mount Yotei.

Hokkaido has a rich assortment of plants, including fruit and nut trees, wild herbs, berries, vegetables, and flowers. The Ainu were experts at using the abundant plant life of their island. They gathered wild vegetables from the forest.

Forest Plants

Forests cover almost 70 percent of Hokkaido. Deciduous trees, or trees that shed their leaves each year, grow in the warm regions. These trees include oak, maple, birch, and elm. Evergreen trees are common in the cold regions. They include fir, spruce, and pine. Mosses, lichens, and dwarf bamboo trees grow on the forest floor.

Below: Wild plants grow in the waters of a Hokkaido lake.

Above: Pink moss covers a Hokkaido hillside.

Trees and Flowers

The Ainu used plants in many ways. They made strong fabric from the bark of elm trees. They used oak trees to build boats and houses. They used birch bark to make household containers and to wrap smoked meats. The Ainu also ate wildflowers, such as wild lilies. They used aconite, a wildflower that contains poison, to make poisonous arrows for hunting.

JEWELS OF THE LAKE

Lake Akan in eastern Hokkaido is home to beautiful sea plants called *marimo* (*right*). They are round like a ball and can grow to be 1 foot (30 centimeters) across. Their surface looks like green velvet. In 1921, the Japanese government declared the plant a national treasure. But people picked marimo in great numbers. By 1940, very few were left. So the Ainu started a program to protect marimo. In 1950, they hosted the first Marimo Festival, held every year in October. At the festival, people honor marimo and learn about ways to protect them.

WILD HOKKAIDO

Above: A raccoon dog sits among fallen autumn leaves.

Hokkaido has a huge variety of wildlife. Birds enjoy the warm waters of Hokkaido's lakes and bays. Mammals make their homes in the forests and rugged mountains. Countless fish and sea mammals swim along the coastline.

Below: Hokkaido's wild boar. Different species of boars are found throughout Japan.

On the Land

Brown bears, foxes, deer, antelope, arctic hares, raccoon dogs, and wild boars are just a few of the animals that roam the forests and mountains of Hokkaido. The brown bear is the largest land mammal in Japan. It lives on Hokkaido but not on the other Japanese islands. It can grow to over 6 feet (1.8 meters) in height and can weigh more than 700 pounds (318 kilograms). The sika, or Japanese deer, is the smallest member of the deer family. It stands only about 34 inches (86 centimeters) tall at the shoulder. The raccoon dog is also tiny. Its face has a dark "mask" like a raccoon's.

In the Water

The waters of Hokkaido are full of life. The deep seas surrounding the island are home to large marine mammals such as whales, walruses, sea lions, seals, and dolphins. Saltwater fishes like herring, mackerel, tuna, sardines, anchovies, cod, salmon, and trout swim along the coast. Shrimp, crabs, oysters, clams, and lobsters are also plentiful. Colorful sea anemones (called sea buttercups) live in the water, too. Hokkaido's rivers and lakes contain trout, perch, and other freshwater fish. In autumn, salmon swim up Hokkaido's rivers to lay their eggs. The ancient Ainu ate a lot of fish, especially salmon.

Above: Swans perform a courtship dance on a frozen lake.

In the Air

Many waterbirds such as gulls, herons, ducks, geese, cranes, and cormorants live on Hokkaido. Eagles, hawks, falcons, and owls hunt other animals for food in the island's forests and waters. Hokkaido is also home to more than 150 species of colorful songbirds. Some birds are very rare, such as the endangered Japanese crane. This elegant bird is the national symbol of Japan.

DANCING CRANES

Japanese cranes (*above*) perform graceful dances when they want to attract mates. These dances are breathtaking, especially when seen against Hokkaido's snowy landscape. The Ainu people honor the cranes with a dance that copies their movements. The cranes are so lovely that the Ainu say the birds are "dressed in clothes from heaven."

THE FIRST AINU

Wwhen scientists from Europe and the United States first met Ainu people in the late 1800s, they were surprised and confused. With their curly hair and pale skin, the Ainu didn't look at all like Japanese people. Some scientists thought the Ainu were related to Europeans, not to the Japanese and other Asians. Most modern scientists think the Ainu are, in fact, related to other Asians. But scientists still disagree on the exact origins of the Ainu.

Above: Ainu men grew long beards.

Ancestors of the Ainu

Scientists aren't sure when the Ainu came to Japan or where they came from. Their ancestors probably arrived many thousands of years ago, traveling over land bridges that once connected Japan to mainland Asia. A lot of Japanese towns, rivers, and mountains have Ainu names. So the Ainu were probably the first people in Japan, naming places before anyone else. Later, the ancestors of the Japanese arrived on the islands. Japanese scrolls created between A.D. 710 and 784 mention people who wore tattoos and practiced the Ainu religion. The Japanese called these people *emishi*, meaning "barbarians."

Above: Lacquerware was an item of trade between the Ainu and the Japanese.

Early Trade

In ancient times, the Ainu lived mainly on Hokkaido. The Japanese lived mainly on Honshu. In the late 1100s, Japanese traders started to travel to Hokkaido from Honshu. The traders brought rice, ceramics, cotton cloth, silk, lacquerware, and iron tools to trade with the Ainu. In exchange, the Ainu gave the Japanese salmon, animal skins, fish oil, eagle feathers, and live hawks, which helped Japanese hunters. The Japanese traders created scrolls containing pictures and written accounts of the Ainu. These records are important to researchers because they show the daily life of the Ainu people in earlier times.

Left: Ainu men greet each other in this photo from the early 1940s.

DESCENDANTS OF THE BEAR

The bear (*below*) is sacred to the Ainu. They call it "the god of the mountain." An ancient Ainu legend tells of a lonely young widow whose husband had died before they had any children. One evening, a man dressed all in black appeared at her hut. He said he was the god of the mountain—the bear—who had come down to Earth in human form. He promised her a son so that she wouldn't be so lonely. He said that her son would grow up to be a mighty hunter and a brave leader of his people. His prediction came true, and the woman lived happily with her son. He is said to be the ancestor of many modern Ainu people.

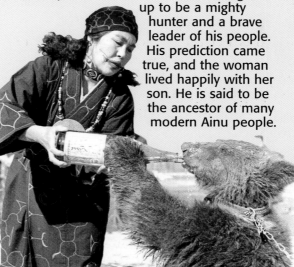

FIGHTING FOR SURVIVAL

During the early 1400s, large numbers of Japanese people began to settle in southern Hokkaido. At first, the Ainu and the Japanese traded and lived peacefully with one another. However, as more Japanese moved into Hokkaido, the new immigrants began to take over Ainu lands. The Ainu got angry. The two groups began to fight. The Ainu fought to preserve their way of life.

Left: An Ainu man dressed as an ancient Ainu warrior

Pushed from Their Lands

The Ainu were not a large group. They did not have a unified nation. They lived in small bands that were independent from one another. This lack of unity made it hard for the Ainu to resist the Japanese settlers. Although the Ainu were skilled fighters, the Japanese gradually pushed them north. Some Ainu fled to the mountains. Others moved to the islands north of Hokkaido. Some groups stayed and tried to fight the Japanese.

Left: A man wears the traditional costume of an ancient Japanese warrior during a festival.

Fighting Back

Between the 1400s and the 1800s, the Ainu fought many wars with the Japanese, trying to preserve their territory. But the Japanese were strong warriors. In every conflict, they defeated the Ainu. Finally, the Ainu fell under Japanese control. The Japanese took the best hunting and fishing territories for themselves. They forced the Ainu to gather in small areas, where there was not enough food and land for everyone. The Japanese forced many Ainu people to work at fishing grounds. There, Japanese bosses treated the Ainu cruelly.

100 pieces of dried salmon

66 pounds (30 kilograms) of rice

22 pounds (10 kilograms) of rice

UNFAIR TRADE

As the Ainu lost their lands and hunting grounds to the Japanese, trading for food became more important to them. They traded dried salmon for rice, which they called "food of the lords." But Japanese rice traders did not always deal fairly with the Ainu. At first, the Ainu traded 100 pieces of dried salmon for 66 pounds (30 kilograms) of rice. But as the years went on, the Japanese offered the Ainu only 22 pounds (10 kilograms) of rice in exchange for the same amount of dried salmon (*left*).

FURTHER STRUGGLES

Shoguns, or military dictators, once ruled small territories all over Japan, including Hokkaido. In 1868, a single Japanese government, headed by an emperor, replaced the many shogun governments. Called the Meiji Restoration (1868–1912), after the name given to the emperor when he took over the throne, this era brought about a period of rapid growth in Japan. However, the Meiji Restoration almost brought an end to Ainu culture.

Above: Emperor Meiji of Japan

Left: When the Japanese claimed Hokkaido for themselves, they took the lands with the best fishing and hunting grounds.

The Claiming of Hokkaido

In 1869, big changes took place in Hokkaido. The Russians had been sending soldiers to Sakhalin Island, north of Hokkaido. Japan feared that the Russians would move into Hokkaido next. The Japanese wanted to secure Hokkaido for themselves. The government offered free farmland to Japanese settlers who moved to Hokkaido. The settlers were given the best land on the island. Life became even more difficult for the Ainu. They were forced to move to rocky, barren lands. The Ainu could no longer hunt and gather food as they had for centuries.

Population Decline

In 1822, according to government surveys, more than 23,000 Ainu lived on Hokkaido. By 1873, the Ainu population had fallen to about 16,000. Poverty, starvation, and disease had claimed many Ainu lives. The Japanese government passed the Former Aborigine Protection Act in 1899. This law was supposed to help the Ainu. But it actually forced the Ainu to live like the Japanese. Under this law, Ainu people were not allowed to practice their native customs, including their religion. Government officials even took away Ainu people's names and gave them Japanese names.

Below: The Notification of Partial Ban on Salmon Fishing limited the areas where the Ainu could catch salmon. The Japanese government issued this document in the late 1800s.

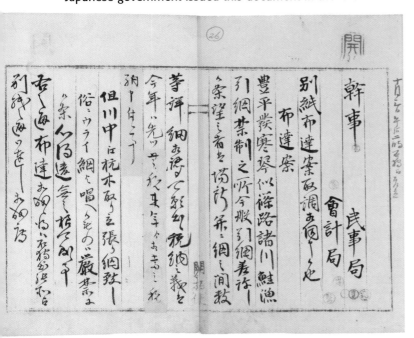

SCHOOL DAYS

Before 1899, the Ainu were forbidden to speak Japanese and practice Japanese customs. The Former Aborigine Protection Act completely reversed this rule. It forced the Ainu to adopt Japanese ways. Ainu children were made to attend Japanese schools. They were forbidden to speak their own language and had to learn Japanese. Soon, many children forgot how to speak Ainu.

KEEPING THE CULTURE ALIVE

People from Europe and North America first learned about the Ainu in the early 1900s. Because the Ainu did not look like other Japanese people, outsiders were curious about them. Tourists began to visit Hokkaido. Some people treated the Ainu more like "wild savages" than human beings. At the St. Louis World's Fair in Missouri in 1904, a group of Ainu were put on display, along with other native people from North and South America, Africa, and Asia.

Below: During World War II, many Japanese homes were destroyed by enemy bombs. Many Japanese refugees fled to Hokkaido.

Poverty and Discrimination

World War II brought great changes to Japan. Many Japanese cities were bombed during the war. Many people lost their homes. When the war ended in 1945, refugees poured into Hokkaido from other parts of Japan and Asia. The island's population increased greatly. Also in 1945, the Russians drove most of the Ainu people from Sakhalin and the Kurile Islands. These people, too, moved to Hokkaido. As the population of Hokkaido grew, jobs became scarce. Many Ainu had very little education. They were unable to find work. Many lived in poverty.

Above: Modern Ainu children dressed in traditional costumes

Hope for the Future

In 1946, Japan became a democratic society. At that time, the Ainu were given full rights as Japanese citizens. But the Ainu wanted the government to help protect and preserve Ainu culture. They formed the Hokkaido Ainu Association in 1946. It worked to provide better educational and social programs for Ainu people. In 1994 a man named Shigeru Kayano became the first Ainu ever elected to the Japanese parliament. In 1997 the Japanese parliament passed the Ainu Shinpo law. This law was designed to protect and preserve Ainu culture.

REVIVING THE ANCIENT TRADITIONS

The Foundation for Research and Promotion of Ainu Culture (FRPAC) was founded in 1997. The foundation has two centers—its headquarters in Sapporo on Hokkaido and the Ainu Culture Center in Tokyo on Honshu. FRPAC has launched many exciting programs, such as Ainu language classes, Ainu festivals, and recitals of Ainu poems.

THE TRADITIONAL ECONOMY

Traditional Ainu life was based upon a subsistence economy. This means that people lived off the land, taking only what they needed to survive. Villagers worked together—hunting, fishing, and gathering food. The ancient Ainu did not use money. They traded for any items that they couldn't get from the land around them.

Right: An Ainu fisherman proudly shows off his catch—a Hokkaido salmon.

Above: This man is catching fish using a traditional Ainu fishing tool.

Hunting Grounds

Hunting and fishing were the backbone of the traditional Ainu economy. Land was valuable. Each village owned a specific area where the people hunted, fished, and gathered wild vegetables and fruits. Sometimes several villages shared hunting grounds. Since the Ainu depended on hunting and fishing for survival, they jealously guarded their territory. People caught trespassing were severely punished and sometimes even killed.

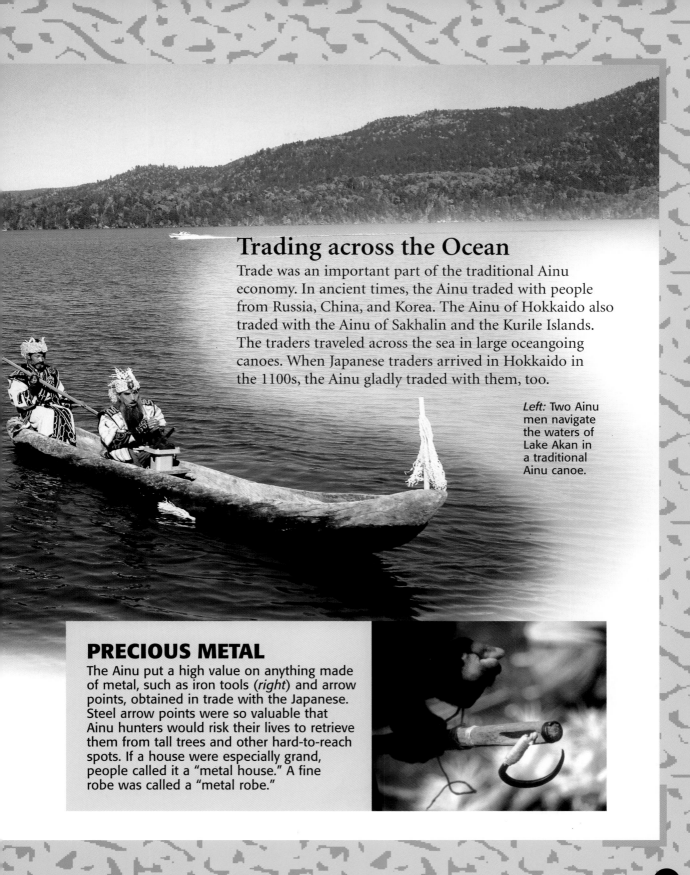

Trading across the Ocean

Trade was an important part of the traditional Ainu economy. In ancient times, the Ainu traded with people from Russia, China, and Korea. The Ainu of Hokkaido also traded with the Ainu of Sakhalin and the Kurile Islands. The traders traveled across the sea in large oceangoing canoes. When Japanese traders arrived in Hokkaido in the 1100s, the Ainu gladly traded with them, too.

Left: Two Ainu men navigate the waters of Lake Akan in a traditional Ainu canoe.

PRECIOUS METAL

The Ainu put a high value on anything made of metal, such as iron tools (*right*) and arrow points, obtained in trade with the Japanese. Steel arrow points were so valuable that Ainu hunters would risk their lives to retrieve them from tall trees and other hard-to-reach spots. If a house were especially grand, people called it a "metal house." A fine robe was called a "metal robe."

THE CHANGING ECONOMY

The Japanese economy grew during the Meiji Restoration. The Japanese took advantage of Hokkaido's rich natural resources. All over Hokkaido, they built factories, fishing ports, and mines. The Japanese cut down ancient forests to make way for farms. With their hunting and fishing grounds gone, many Ainu took jobs as loggers, factory workers, construction workers, and farmhands.

The Fishing Ban

During the Meiji Restoration, the Japanese fishing industry thrived. Fishing crews used giant nets to scoop huge numbers of fish from the sea. But while many Japanese fishermen grew wealthy, Ainu fishermen were restricted. A new law said that the Ainu could fish only on certain days and in certain locations. The law set strict limits on how many salmon an Ainu fisherman could catch. People who broke the fishing law were taken to prison.

Left: Many modern Ainu men have found jobs as woodcarvers.

Money Becomes a Necessity

The Meiji Restoration brought modern conveniences, such as roads, railways, and post offices, to Hokkaido. Construction companies hired Ainu men to build houses, bridges, and roads. These jobs gave many Ainu people their first experience with money. But most Ainu were paid much lower wages than their Japanese coworkers. Many couldn't pay their bills. They grew in debt to Japanese merchants. They sometimes had to sell their homes and possessions. Children went hungry. Some Ainu children were sent to live with relatives. Others were put up for adoption.

The Struggle to Succeed

In modern times, fishing, forestry, and farming are still important industries in Hokkaido. Many Ainu still work in these businesses. But modern Ainu also work in nearly all other fields, including teaching, business, and politics.

Above: The Ainu Village in Hokkaido attracts many tourists every year.

ARTS AND TOURISM

Many tourists visit Hokkaido to fish or to hike in the scenic mountains. Some Ainu work as nature guides, showing tourists the beauty of their island. Other Ainu teach visitors about their culture. They work in museums and cultural centers (*right*). Ainu musicians, singers, and dancers perform at cultural festivals. Ainu woodcarvers, textile artists, and other craftspeople earn a living selling their work to tourists, art collectors, and art galleries.

TRADITIONAL HOMES

Ainu villages, or *kotan*, were located near water. The kotan were small, with just four to seven families in each village. Each family lived in its own home. Most present-day Ainu live in modern apartments. However, the Hokkaido government has recently built replicas of Ainu villages to help people learn about the traditional Ainu way of life.

Above: A traditional Ainu storehouse

Below: The Ainu believed that the sacred hedge outside their homes protected them from disaster and evil spirits.

Small and Simple

Ainu homes were small but sturdy. The Ainu used natural materials, such as tree trunks, grasses, and tree bark, to build their homes. Each home had a fireplace that was used for cooking, heating, and lighting. A sacred platform called an *iyoykir* held valuable items, such as hunting tools and containers.

Above: Modern Ainu women inside a traditional-style Ainu home

The Spirit of the House

In the northeastern corner of every Ainu home stood the *inaw*, or spirit of the house. The inaw was made of a willow stick hung with curls of shaved willow. In the center of the inaw was the "heart"—a notched section that held a piece of burning coal on special occasions. The inaw was the first thing the owners set up in any new home.

Outside the Homes

Many Ainu villages had a sacred hedge on the eastern side of the homes. The hedge was made of many large inaw stuck into the ground. It was meant to please the gods and protect the homes from evil spirits. Each village also had drying racks for fish and plants and a storage house for food. Every village also had several outdoor altars, used during religious rituals.

NO PEEKING!

Most Ainu homes had three windows. The most important was the *rorun puyar*, or sacred window. It was always located on the eastern side of the house, facing the sacred hedge. The Ainu used the rorun puyar to pass sacred objects, used in religious ceremonies, in and out of the home. The Ainu believed the window also allowed gods to enter and leave the house. Since this window was sacred, the Ainu were forbidden to look through it like an ordinary window.

MODERN HOMES

Modern Ainu homes vary in style. Most present-day Ainu live in the same types of homes as the Japanese. These homes include high-rise apartment buildings. However, some Ainu live in traditional-style villages that have been built in recent years. These villages are open to tourists who want to learn more about Ainu culture.

Village Abandoned

When the Japanese took over Ainu lands, they also took over many Ainu villages. They forced the Ainu in these villages to work for them as farmhands and fishermen. When the Japanese had used up all the natural resources near the villages, they moved on and forced the Ainu to relocate with them. Soon, many Ainu villages were deserted.

Below: Some modern-day Ainu villages serve as tourist attractions where the Ainu demonstrate their crafts and sell souvenirs.

New Ainu Villages

With the support of the Hokkaido government, some traditional Ainu villages have been reproduced. One example is located at the Ainu Museum in Shiraoi. It is a beautiful and realistic copy of an old village that once stood on the same site. A 52-foot (15.8-meter) wooden statue of the village leader greets visitors at the village entrance. He holds a sacred inaw and prays for the safety and happiness of visitors. Guests are treated to demonstrations of traditional Ainu handicrafts, festivals, and everyday life.

Above: An Ainu girl in traditional dress greets visitors to her shop in the Ainu Village in Hokkaido.

Museum Exhibits

Museums around the world display traditional Ainu homes, outbuildings, canoes, and household items. Ainu art, both traditional and modern, is often displayed. So are Ainu tools and weapons. Sometimes Ainu performers in traditional robes entertain and educate visitors. The Smithsonian Institution in Washington, D.C., has held successful Ainu folk festivals and exhibits.

WINTER SECLUSION

In northern Hokkaido, heavy snowfall (*right*) blocks many mountain passes for up to six months a year. Because of the snow, Ainu people who live in the north cannot travel to and from their villages. They must prepare for the cold winter months just as their ancestors did many centuries ago. They fill storage houses with dried meats and vegetables. They often store fish they have caught beneath frozen rivers and lakes.

VILLAGE LIFE

Above: An Ainu man performs the bow and arrow dance during a festival.

In the past, strict laws governed Ainu village life. Status was very important. The elderly had the highest status because the Ainu thought that elderly people were closest to the spirit world. Men usually ranked higher than women. But elderly women ranked higher than young men. The Ainu also had well-defined gender roles. Men did only men's work, and women did only women's work.

Village Leaders

Below: Ainu village elders pray to the gods during a religious ceremony.

Each village had a chief, a council of elders, and a shaman, or spiritual leader. The chief was a man with outstanding abilities, such as military or hunting skills. The council of elders usually elected the chief, although the job was sometimes inherited— passed down from father to son. The chief and the council of elders settled disputes within the village. The village shaman could be either male or female. Often, the shaman was a woman, since the Ainu believed women were closer to the spirit world than men.

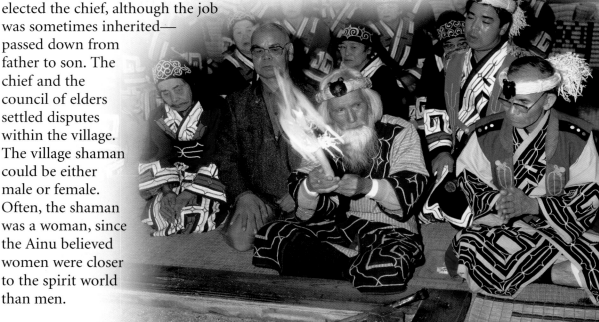

Ainu Girls and Women

At a young age, Ainu girls learned to help their mothers with household chores. This work included drying meat, gathering plants, cooking, sewing, and grinding grain with large, heavy stones. Girls were considered adults at fifteen or sixteen years of age and were then allowed to marry. Parents arranged some marriages, but most young women were allowed to choose their own husbands.

Above: According to Ainu tradition, women sat separately from men during festivities.

Naming the Baby

Ainu babies were considered gifts from heaven. To protect babies from illness (thought to be caused by evil spirits), parents didn't name children until they were two or three years old. Before that, babies had nicknames, such as Ayay ("baby's cry"). Most permanent names described the child's behavior or appearance. Traditionally, Ainu people didn't have first and last names. They had only one name.

Ainu Boys and Men

Ainu men were excellent archers. Boys played with tiny bows and arrows, learning to become good hunters. A favorite game involved shooting objects off other boys' heads with arrows. This game was a test of bravery and skill. Boys were considered adults when they reached fifteen or sixteen years of age. They could marry at age seventeen or eighteen. A young man interested in marrying a woman first made a formal visit to her home. The woman gave him a bowl of cooked rice. He ate half of it and then handed the bowl back to her. If she finished the rice in the bowl, it meant she had accepted his proposal.

TOKENS OF AFFECTION

Ainu men and women carried small knives called *makiri.* The blades were usually made of ivory and were 4 to 6 inches (10 to 15 centimeters) long. The sheaths, or cases, were made of ivory, maple, walnut, cherry, or another fine wood. Knives and sheaths were intricately carved. When a boy made an especially beautiful makiri, he gave it to a special girl as a courtship gift.

THE BEAR HUNTERS

The Ainu got most of their food by hunting and fishing. Men usually hunted in small groups, using trained dogs to help track game. Women sometimes went on hunting trips but only to carry baggage and cook meals. Strong women who could carry heavy loads were highly valued as wives.

Important Animals

Ainu men proudly called themselves bear hunters, but they mostly hunted deer. They also hunted foxes, raccoon dogs, antelope, and arctic hares. These animals provided people with meat, furs, and skins.

Fishing

The Ainu fished for trout in summer and salmon in fall, plus many other fish year-round. The Ainu also hunted whales and seals. They used spears, traps, and harpoons.

Left: Ainu women usually did not go out fishing or hunting. They worked in the home, cooking the meals and weaving cloth.

Gathering Wild Plants

The Ainu also gathered wild plants for food. They combined vegetables, such as wild carrots, turnips, and onions, with animal fat and water to make soup. Garlic soup was a favorite dish in early spring. Vegetables were also eaten raw. In summer, the Ainu picked berries, fruits, and wild grains. In autumn, they picked nuts and mushrooms. They dried some of these foods and stored them away for the cold winter months.

Left: An Ainu woman holds a plate of pears to be offered to the gods.

Grains and Grasses

Ainu people made porridge, cereal, and dumplings from a variety of grains. They picked wild grains and grasses. They also grew small fields of millet, wheat, buckwheat, and grasses. Women and children did the planting and harvesting, using very simple farming methods. They scattered seeds onto cleared land and left the plants to grow. To harvest the grains, they simply plucked the heads off the stalks using an oyster shell.

Right: Ainu meals included porridge mixed with grain and edible wild plants.

HUNTING WITH POISON

Ainu men often used poison arrows to kill large animals like bears. The poison came from a plant called aconite. Making poison was a specialty—families had their own carefully guarded recipes. Hunters also used spring-loaded poison traps, usually placed along animal trails and set between two trees. The Japanese government outlawed the use of poison arrows and traps in 1904.

CLOTHING FOR ALL SEASONS

The Ainu made clothing from a wide variety of plant and animal materials. They used deerskin, bird skins, fish skins, and feathers to make lightweight robes and shoes. They used animal fur to make warm capes, leggings, and gloves. The most common piece of Ainu clothing was a robe, similar to a Japanese kimono. It was made from bark and plant fibers.

Working with Fur

Ainu women made warm clothing out of bear, rabbit, fox, sable, and raccoon dog fur. Bear furs were usually left in one piece and were worn over the shoulders like a cape. Gloves were made from the skins of smaller animals. Ainu women were experts at preparing fur and skins. Japanese traders prized the soft, flexible animal skins made by the Ainu and often traded cotton for them.

Right: An Ainu man dressed in full festival attire, wearing a wood fiber crown

Special Clothes

The Ainu wore elegant robes on special occasions. The robes were made of small pieces of dyed and white cotton, sewn together like a quilt. People in different regions decorated their robes differently. For instance, those who lived by the sea decorated their robes with designs of marine animals, such as killer whales. Ainu who lived in the forest made owl and tree designs. The robes usually had colored cloth cutouts at the collar, cuffs, and hem. The Ainu believed that these cutouts protected the wearer from evil spirits. Modern Ainu still wear these robes on special occasions.

Above: An Ainu robe made of bark fibers

Ornaments

Ornaments were a sign of wealth and status for the Ainu. Women wore embroidered headbands and beaded necklaces and bracelets. Both men and women wore earrings and carried makiri knives. For special occasions, Ainu men wore crowns made of wood fibers. Most chiefs wore crowns all the time. Each crown had a carved wooden ornament at the center—usually the image of an animal god. Men also wore long swords at their waists.

BEAUTY MARKS

Ainu women painted tattoos on their faces, arms, and hands, starting at the age of twelve or thirteen. The face tattoo was made first on a small section of the face and then made larger each year. When finished, the tattoo looked a little like a mustache (*left*). Arms and hands were tattooed with lines, dots, and circles. The dye used for tattooing was a bright blue-green that never faded. It was made from soot and ash tree bark. The tattoos were usually completed by fifteen or sixteen years of age. The young women were then eligible for marriage.

THE ART OF THE AINU

Nature provided the Ainu with art supplies and design ideas. Artists used mostly wood and natural fibers as materials. Animals and plants were the most popular designs. The ancient Ainu decorated almost everything they owned, from household tools to special robes. The artwork included flowing and geometric patterns. The Ainu never drew pictures of people, however. They believed that to capture a person's face was to capture his or her spirit.

Woodcarvers

Ainu men were famous for their woodcarving skills. They carved tools and household utensils that were useful and beautiful. In ancient times, the Ainu performed special ceremonies before beginning to work. Before chopping down a tree, for instance, Ainu craftsmen praised the tree for its beauty and explained what they were going to make from it. Some modern Ainu woodcarvers still practice this ancient ritual. Carvings of bears are the most popular among tourists and art collectors.

Right: An Ainu woodcarver at work

Above: An Ainu woman plays the mukkuri.

Musicians

Ainu musicians play various instruments. The *tonkori* is a stringed instrument similar to a banjo. The *mukkuri* is made from a strip of bamboo. The player holds the mukkuri between his or her teeth and vibrates a thin flap cut into the center of the instrument by pulling a string. Musicians also bang on drums and container lids. The Mukkuri Ensemble is a group of modern Ainu musicians who play traditional instruments and perform traditional Ainu songs and dances.

Writers

In the early 1900s, Ainu writers began recording their history in books. But the Ainu had no written language of their own. So the writers usually wrote in English or Japanese. Before he was elected to the Japanese parliament, Shigeru Kayano, an Ainu man, wrote *Our Land Was a Forest: An Ainu Memoir.* In this book, he wrote about the poverty of his childhood, his struggles to make a living as a young man, and the movement to revive Ainu culture. Other Ainu writers have created beautiful, moving poems about their struggles.

Below: Shigeru Kayano is the first Ainu to be elected to the Japanese Diet, or parliament.

TRADITION AND INNOVATION

Noriko Kawamura is a modern Ainu textile artist. She makes beautiful wall hangings and traditional gowns. Her work was shown at the 1996 Smithsonian Folklife Festival. It helped spark interest in Ainu culture in the United States. Kawamura creates her pieces from a wide variety of natural materials. Her work displays classic Ainu patterns with a modern twist.

THE ANCIENT LANGUAGE OF THE AINU

The Ainu language shares some words with Japanese. Mount Fuji, the tallest mountain in Japan, may have gotten its name from the Ainu word *huchi*, which means "fire." Speakers can change the meaning of Ainu words by adding suffixes, or special endings. For example, adding the suffix *-ya* turns a phrase into a question. The traditional Ainu language was spoken only. The Ainu had no written language.

A Forbidden Language

In 1899, the Japanese banned the use of the Ainu language. In school, Ainu children were forced to speak Japanese. The spoken Ainu language began to disappear. By 1979, only about ten Ainu could still speak their native tongue. A growing interest in Ainu culture has recently revived the language.

Right: These Ainu girls, like other children of Ainu descent, speak only Japanese.

Preserving the Language

Even though people were not allowed to speak Ainu, scholars wanted to preserve the language. In the late 1800s and early 1900s, foreigners began to write down the Ainu language using their own alphabets. One Englishman created an Ainu dictionary. Many Ainu and non-Ainu wrote down Ainu folktales in English and Japanese. Most modern Ainu writing is done in Japanese.

Left: Many books about the Ainu language and culture are written in Japanese.

The Oral Tradition

The Ainu preserved their history through stories. Ainu storytellers were highly respected. *Yukar*, or long tales of heroes (both humans and gods), were the most popular stories. Yukar were called "grandmother tales" because women passed the stories down to their daughters by word of mouth. *Kamui yukar* were exciting tales of Ainu gods.

Below: An Ainu woman recites a yukar.

Words of Power

Words had great power to the ancient Ainu. They believed that people could curse one another to death with evil words. However, if a man made a mistake when he was cursing another, the words could backfire and destroy him and his family. In earlier eras, the Ainu settled disputes with debates that went on for days. Two men would argue until one either dropped out from exhaustion or could think of nothing more to say. The best speaker was usually the winner.

RECORDING THE OLD TALES

Matsu Kannari, named Ikameno in Ainu, lived from 1875 to 1961. Using the English alphabet, she began writing down Ainu yukar in 1928. Before she died, Kannari recorded ninety-two stories from memory. She was the first Ainu to put yukar into writing. The Japanese government gave her special medals for her work.

THE WORLD OF SPIRITS

The ancient Ainu believed that the world was filled with spirits—both good and evil. The Ainu believed that gods lived inside everything, from the mighty bear to the lowly cooking pot. The belief that gods inhabit everyday things is called animism. Some Ainu people still practice their traditional religion.

Right: An Ainu elder holds a bowl filled with liquor during a ceremony. Men use the stick over the bowl to keep their beards out of the bowl when they take a drink.

Animal Gods

The most important god in the Ainu religion was the bear. He was called *chira mante kamuy*—"king of the mountain gods." He lived in heaven but visited the Earth disguised as a bear. If he was pleased with the people, he did them no harm. But if the humans angered him, he went on a rampage, raiding the village storage hut and killing people. The owl was considered the "guardian of the forest." The killer whale was called "king of the sea gods."

Talking to the Gods

According to Ainu traditional belief, people depended on gods for food, help, and protection. The gods also depended upon humans for status and wealth. Communication with the gods was essential. Shamans acted as messengers between gods and people.

Right: Ainu men bow down as a sign of respect to the gods before drinking sacred liquor at a festival.

Sending the Spirits Back

After killing an animal for food, the Ainu sent the animal's spirit back to heaven in a special "sending back" ritual. They offered the animal gifts, such as rice wine and millet cakes. When the animal's spirit returned to heaven, it showed the other gods the gifts from the people and shared its food and wine. When the other gods heard of his respectful treatment from humans, they too wanted to visit Earth and offer themselves to the people.

THE HEAD-STRIKING WOOD

Ainu fishermen used a thick willow stick called a *isapa kik ni*, or head-striking wood (*left*) to kill salmon. An ancient legend says that long ago, humans killed salmon with rotted wood or any tool that was handy. The salmon god felt that the fishermen were being disrespectful. He was angry and refused to visit Earth. The people couldn't find any salmon, and they began to starve. The salmon god said that fishermen must use only isapa kik ni to kill salmon. When they did, the salmon returned. Some modern Ainu fishermen still use isapa kik ni to kill salmon.

AINU FESTIVALS

Traditional Ainu festivals revolved around nature and religion. At some festivals, people asked the gods for blessings. The Ainu also held festivals when illness or disaster struck. These festivals were very noisy. People banged on drums and clashed swords to scare away the evil spirits that had brought them misfortune.

Above: Women sing at a Bear Festival.

Below: In modern Bear Festival celebrations, Ainu do not kill the bears during the ceremony but use them only for the ritual singing and dancing.

The Traditional Bear Festival

The Iyomante, or Bear Festival, was the most sacred Ainu festival. People prepared for the festival years in advance. They captured a very young bear cub and tenderly cared for it in a special cage. The festival was held in January or February. Many Ainu villages gathered together for the celebration, which lasted three days. The host village worked hard before the festival, cutting fresh inaw as a gift to the bear's spirit, brewing millet beer and rice wine, and making millet cakes. Then the bear cub was killed in a special ceremony. People shared the meat in a big feast. The Ainu still celebrate the Bear Festival but they no longer kill bear cubs.

Above: Since the Ainu no longer kill bears during the festivals, they usually place a replica of a bear's hide on the altar, along with food offerings.

The Modern Salmon Festival

The ancient Ainu held the Salmon Festival to honor the return of the salmon in fall. Modern Ainu still hold this festival in many cities on Hokkaido. The festival is a lot of fun. People sing and dance, while traditional music fills the air. Visitors watch traditional Ainu fishing demonstrations. They eat freshly caught salmon, cooked in traditional ways. Visitors also watch Ainu craftspeople make handicrafts and can purchase them as souvenirs. Games and contests are plentiful. In one game, people try to catch slippery salmon with their bare hands.

THE BEAR FESTIVAL ON FILM

In the early 1930s, Dr. Neil Gordon Munro, a Scottish doctor who lived among the Ainu, filmed a traditional Bear Festival, held in the Saru River district of Hokkaido. The film is considered a precious historical record of Ainu culture.

SONG AND DANCE

Above: Traditionally, only men performed the bow and arrow dance. Women were not allowed to hold weapons.

Traditional Ainu festivals always included dancing and singing. The dances and songs were not simply a form of entertainment but were part of religious rituals. The Ainu danced and sang to communicate with the gods. Many dances imitated activities like hunting or the movements of animals like the bear. Songs often told stories of ancient times.

Below: Women perform a traditional dance at the Ainu Museum in Shiraoi, Hokkaido.

The Bear Festival Dance

The Bear Festival dance was the Ainu's most sacred dance. Participants started dancing a few at a time. They began slowly, imitating the movements of the bear. More dancers joined in, creating a big circle. They danced faster and faster, in a whirl of singing and stomping. The Ainu still perform this dance during the Bear Festival.

Above: Two women perform the crane dance.

Fun and Games

Many Ainu festivals involve dance contests. In one contest, the last person left dancing is the winner. Onlookers laugh and shout to encourage the competitors to keep dancing. In another contest, Ainu women toss a serving tray back and forth, in time to the music. The tossing becomes faster and faster. Women are eliminated one by one when they drop the tray.

Festival Songs

Singing is an important part of Ainu festivals. To start the festivities, women sit in a circle and sing, while beating on container lids. For festivals of celebration, women sing happy songs. During times of sadness, such as funerals, they wail songs of sorrow. Some festival songs are epic poems—long poems about heroic acts. One person sings or chants the poem. Other singers join in on the chorus and set a rhythm by tapping sticks or stomping their feet.

Storytelling

At the close of ancient festivals, people told yukar around the fire. The storytelling often went on late into the night. Children fell asleep, snuggled on the laps of their mothers, with tales of heroes and gods filling their dreams. The old tales not only brought a restful close to the festivities but also kept Ainu traditions alive.

THE SWORD DANCE

The Ainu sword dance is performed only by men. It is a spine-tingling display of courage and skill. Spectators shout encouragement as the whirling dancers clash their swords together violently. The men mimic fighting to scare away evil spirits. The sword dance is still performed at many museums and restored Ainu villages.

GLOSSARY

aconite: a plant belonging to the buttercup family. Some species of aconite can be used to make poison or medicine.

ainu (**EYE-noo**): the Ainu word for human beings

Ainu Moshir (EYE-noo moh-SHEER): the Ainu name for their homeland

anemone: a sea animal related to the coral and jellyfish. Most sea anemones resemble flowers.

animism: the belief that spirits inhabit animals, plants, and everyday objects

discriminate: to treat a group of people unfairly because of prejudice or hatred

endangered: in danger of becoming extinct

epic poems: long poems recounting the deeds of legendary or historical figures

inaw (**ee-NOW**): a wooden stick with attached wood shavings at the top. The inaw is used as an offering to the gods.

inherited: passed down from one generation to the next

kotan (**koh-TAHN**): an Ainu village or community

marimo (**mah-REE-moh**): a sea plant that resembles a small, green velvet ball

mukkuri (**MOOK-koo-ree**): a musical instrument made from a strip of bamboo. The mukkuri is found in many other Asian and Oceanian cultures.

refugees: people who flee to a new land, usually to escape danger or cruel treatment

replica: a copy of something

shaman: a priest or priestess who uses magic to cure the sick, tell the future, or influence future events

shogun: a Japanese military governor

subsistence economy: an economic system in which people obtain only the basics needed for survival

suffix: a special ending that changes a word's meaning

yukar (**yoo-KAHR**): tales of gods and legendary characters that were passed down from mothers to daughters by word of mouth

FINDING OUT MORE

Books

Fitzhugh, William, and Chisato O. Dubreuil. *Ainu: Spirit of a Northern People*. Seattle: University of Washington Press, 2000.

Japan in Pictures. Minneapolis: Lerner Publications Co., 1994.

Kayano, Shigeru. *Our Land Was a Forest: An Ainu Memoir*. Translated by Kyoko Selden. Boulder, San Francisco, Oxford: Westview Press, 1994.

Namioka, Lensey. *The Coming of the Bear*. New York: HarperCollins Children's Books, 1992.

San Souci, Robert D. *The Silver Charm*. Illustrated by Yoriko Ito. New York: Doubleday, 2001.

Starr, Frederick. *The Ainu Group at the St. Louis Exposition*. Chicago: The Open Court Publishing Co., 1904.

Videos

Geography 2000: Japan. Education 2000, Inc., 2000.

Lords of Hokkaido. Nature Archive Series, 1986.

Websites

<http://ramat.ram.ne.jp/itak/eng/aisatu.htm>

<http://www.members.iex.net/~mcgarity/sap/index.htm>

<http://www.outdoorjapan.com/aghokkaido1.html>

<http://www.pbs.org/wgbh/nova/hokkaido/migration.html>

<http://www.pref.hokkaido.jp/kseikatu/ks-kknen/text/home/e-index.htm#jouten>

Organizations

Cultural Survival
215 Prospect Street
Cambridge, MA 02139
(617) 441-5400
E-mail: csinc@cs.org
Website: <http://www.cs.org/>

The Foundation for Research and Promotion of Ainu Culture
7F, Presto 1-7, N-1, W-7, Chuo-ku
Sapporo, Hokkaido 060-0001, Japan
(81) 11-271-4171
Website: <http://www.frpac.or.jp/english/frpac/frpac.html>

INDEX

ABOUT THE AUTHOR

Barbara Aoki Poisson was born in Fukuoka, Japan. As the daughter of an American military man, she traveled extensively with her family throughout her childhood. She has lived in Japan, Germany, and eleven states in the United States. Barbara is one-half Japanese and enjoys the many benefits of a multicultural family. Her work has appeared in a variety of national magazines, and she is a regular contributor to *Family Fun*. She's currently at work on several more books for children. Barbara is forever grateful to her supportive family for their assistance and encouragement.

PICTURE CREDIT

(B=bottom; C=center; F= far; I=inset; L=left; M=main; R=right; T=top)

Axiom Photographic Library: 4M, 7TL, 18M, 24BL, 25TL, 46BR • Bruce Coleman Collection: 2TC, 8BL, 9M, 11TR, 12TL, 12–13M, 13TL • Getty Images/Hulton Archive: 9I, 14TL, 14–15M, 15I, 20M • Haga Library Inc., Japan: 3BR, 7I, 8TR, 10TL, 11I, 15TL, 16M, 21TL, 22–23M, 26–27M, 26TR, 27TR, 29I, 30TR, 30–31M, 31TR, 32M, 33TL, 33CR, 35TR, 35I, 37TL, 39I, 40M, 41TR, 42–43M, 42TR, 43TR, 44–45M, 44TL, 45TL • Historical Museum of Hokkaido: 17I, 19M, 39TL • Kyodo News: 37CR • Jean-Philippe Soule/Native Planet Organisation: 22TL, 23I, 41I • Times Editions: 5I, 13I, 18TR • Topham Picturepoint: 6M, 10–11M, 17TL, 28M, 29TL, 34M • Winston Fraser: 22BR, 25I, 36M, 38M